Handbook on Automobiles

Life Lessons for New Drivers

Karen Park and John Milo Beranek

ISBN-10: 1517760321
ISBN-13: 978-1517760328

Karen Park and John Milo Beranek

CONTENTS

FOREWORD

This book started in 2014 when your Uncle Milo and I were driving back from Richmond, Virginia in the 2004 Mazda 6 wagon. You may recall spending a week in this car from your age 13 U.P. trip. We can't know if the Mazda 6 will last until Tedi and Jessie have their trip with us. Currently it has 179,000 miles on it for God's sake.

We don't even know if there will still be cars when you read this book. We are banking on it so this book will have practical use as a handbook of sorts. Remember, we know your parents pretty well, and we know car stuff is not something they will pass on to you. The future possibilities for transportation are really endless and no one can imagine it now. The University of Michigan has just opened a model city for testing autonomous (driverless) cars. Tesla just released a software update to upgrade the Model S to have autonomous function. Yet even if cars are irrelevant in your world, the things we have learned so far could be of use to you in other ways.

The irony with Milo is that even though his career has been in the automobile industry, he believes the world would be a better place without them, or at least not so many.

Milo and I grew up differently when it comes to cars. Milo was into cars when he was five years old. There was a neighbor who had a nice car and Milo remembers looking out his window and watching him work on it. His godfather Ron Stupka was into all kinds of fast cars, including Corvettes. Milo grew up watching older teenagers in his neighborhood working on their cars and sometimes he knew more than they did. He was used to people working on their cars. I never saw anyone work on a car until I met Milo.

I did not drive a car to high school. A few kids in my neighborhood did, but it was unusual. I took the yellow school bus. Milo had a car about as soon as he got his driver's license. It was a 15 year old 1968 Ford Torino GT fastback. It was almost as old as he was. He drove it to high school pretty much every day; he never took the school bus. Before he had his own car, he begged rides to school from his older sister Kara. I believe it was his own idea to get a car, not his parents.

As for me, I went to college and medical school without a car until the second year of medical school. I took public transportation called the "T" in Boston or walked. In my first year of medical school in Richmond, Virginia, I rented an apartment in a house in the Fan on Stuart Avenue and took the city bus down West Broad Street to lectures. Milo left his Torino in his parent's driveway when he first went away to college, but he took cars with him to college in his junior and senior year. Many in my extended family don't own a car and they are grownups with their families and some of them are even grandparents. They live in big cities like New York City, Paris, Seoul, and Hong Kong. So don't feel like you need to own a car.

This handbook mixes practical topics about automobiles with stories about me and Milo and cars. We are writing this book for our nieces and nephews, but the advice applies to all new drivers. Maybe one of you will pass this book onward to another generation. That would be cool.

1 DRIVING

Congratulations, you have driven a car for the first time. Some day you will tell a story about your first drive. My first drive was with my dad in a Volvo station wagon and I drove it around the cul de sac adjacent to our house. I felt really small, just barely able to see over the wheel and reach the gas pedal. The steering was really stiff and I could not steer the car to follow the edge of the road around the circle. Luckily there were no curbs that I could hit and I remember driving counterclockwise.

Milo's first drive is harder to reckon. Milo worked on cars long before he could drive and he regularly had to move cars in and out of his family's driveway in order to work on them. Can you imagine that? So hard to say what was the first drive for him but he remembers driving either the 1974 Ford Pinto or the 1979 Chevy Caprice Classic with his dad and sister Kara in the car. He overshot a turn into the opposite lane such that oncoming traffic was headed straight into them. The oncoming car had to swerve to avoid them. Everybody gasped. Notice that the model year of the car is important to Milo. He insisted on my including the model year of the cars in this book. I have no idea what model year any of my family's cars were.

My advice about learning to drive includes one thing that I only realized after turning 50 years old. Use the passenger side mirror. Get used to looking into it. I never use it and I should. So please learn to use it right away. Use it to parallel park so you can see how far you are from the curb as well as looking at traffic around you.

I also recommend listening to the car without the radio on once in a while. Just listen to the car running. When you know the regular sounds the car makes, you can hear when something is wrong. If you hear a funny sound, listen for when you hear it. It's kind of like listening to the heartbeat with a stethoscope. You can determine if the sound happens when the car is moving or standing still. Then you can listen if it happens when you apply the brakes or when you accelerate. If it happens with a regular rhythm, it could be related to the rotation of the wheels. Then you can listen for which quadrant you hear it the loudest, i.e., the right front, left front, right rear, or left rear. Even if you are not going to fix the car yourself, this information will be very helpful to your mechanic.

Lastly, I have advice for when it is hard to see the road, for example, in weather like heavy rain or snow. This also applies when it is nighttime and oncoming traffic with headlights makes it hard to see. Or even when you feel intimidated by a large truck you are trying to get past on the highway. When you find yourself in this situation, look up the road to the course you want to follow. Don't look at the oncoming headlights. Keep your eyes looking way up the road ahead.

Milo has more driving advice. He says he sees people do these things wrong every day and it drives him crazy.

1. Pay attention to driving when you are driving
   No cell phone, texting, or whatever it is you do at your age. Driving is a responsibility.

2. Four way stop sign
   The first person stopped goes. If two cars stop at exactly the same time, the car on the right goes first. If you are already stopped and other cars are approaching from other directions, you do not have to wait for them to stop before you go through the intersection. Milo says, "Pay attention as you approach the stop sign, and note the arrival order of the other vehicles."

3. Merging to enter traffic
    Accelerate to integrate with moving traffic. Use the merge lane to accelerate. Do not cut in too quickly. Do not cross the solid white lines.

4. Merging from three to two lanes
    Use the entire length of the third lane. Do not merge too early. Maintain your speed and keep traffic flowing. Don't be the jerk that speeds by cars in the other lanes. You'll find that if you drive about the same speed as the other drivers, they won't get angry.

5. Driving in the left lane
    Drive in left lane only when going faster than the right lane. Use the lane for passing. Note, this does not apply when traffic is jam-packed.

When you are comfortable driving automatic transmission, we recommend you learn to drive stick shift, also called manual transmission. We are the only people with stick shift cars in the family. However, Milo and I, Milo's dad and mom, Paul and Kara, my brother John, and Chong know how to drive stick. It is nice to know how. At this time in Europe car rentals are almost all stick shift. Milo does not remember the first time he drove stick shift or who taught him. He feels as though he always knew how. This is very strange because everyone remembers learning stick shift because it involves a lot of lurching and stalling before you can know how to work the clutch. My brother John taught me when I was about twenty-two years old and he was sixteen. You will be surprised when your younger siblings can teach you something.

Driving in good weather is best for new drivers but you might find yourself having to fend for yourself soon when the weather is not perfect. We as Ann Arborites are used to driving in bad weather, mainly snow and ice. But snow is a problem south of here even more so because the roads aren't cleared as quickly and people aren't so comfortable driving in the snow. So this information could help you as well. The best to worst handling cars in inclement weather are as follows: all-wheel drive, four wheel drive, front wheel drive and rear wheel drive. Low ground clearance is also a factor when the snow on the road gets higher than the bottom of the car. In Ann Arbor my rear wheel drive car has failed to make it up inclines twice. Even worse, in Virginia I have been in cars twice that lost traction going over a hill and then slid backwards into ditches. Once in New Hampshire Milo was driving a rear wheel drive car on the highway in the rain and the temperature was getting lower and lower, when he felt a slight shimmy in the rear of the car. He thought that it was strange so he slowed down. Then just over the top of the next hill, he saw cars strewn all over the place. He was okay because he had slowed down.

By the way, many SUVs are all wheel drive and that helps in bad weather, however, they also have a high center of gravity so they are prone to rolling over. So Milo does not recommend buying an SUV for driving in snow. Many people think an SUV is great to drive in the snow and with this false sense of security they are not as careful as they should be. Because of this, the vehicle is more prone to getting out of control.

Driving in snow is usually not a problem, it is the ice that gets you. Tires actually get pretty good traction in snow, kind of like on loose dirt or sand. In snow, drive slower than normal but keep momentum for hills. Don't drive too slow. If you do, you won't make it up hills. Don't be afraid to let the tires slip and slide a bit. The car will seem at first to be out of your control, but in truth sliding a bit in snow is a very controlled behavior. Momentum is your friend, but remember you have very limited ability to brake. Now cars have ABS (antilock braking) and traction control, and stability control, which can make people feel invincible. These technologies will help a bit when you're moving, however, if stuck in snow, traction control is not helpful. So if you are stuck in snow, turn it off. ABS braking is also bad in snow in general because it will take longer to stop with ABS on.

As for the ice, not much you can do to keep the car under control. Tires have very little grip, or friction, on ice. Putting on the brakes doesn't help. A phenomena I never heard of until I came to Michigan is called "black ice." It means you can't see the ice because is it looks dark, like the color of the road. You just have to know that when you are on ice you cannot change direction or slow down. Don't try to because that will set you worse. The best thing to do is just let off the gas gently, keep the steering wheel straight, and let the car slow down on its own. Of course that's assuming you are not headed into a brick wall or another car. Just remember to take it slow and easy when the weather turns ugly.

Rain can also be trouble. As I'm writing, in August 2015 there was a big rainstorm in Ann Arbor. The streets were flooded and running like a fast moving stream with empty trash and recycle bins floating in the roads. Cars were dodging the bins to keep moving through the road. I had a de-ja vu moment remembering thirty years prior when I drove my Honda CRX through a flooded intersection that I couldn't tell how deep the water was. It was so deep that the car slowly stopped. So here's a lesson. What did I do? I opened the car door and the water was so high it filled up the car. Maybe I should have lowered the window if I wanted to get out, or maybe I should have just waited in the car until the water level fell. It was a mistake to open the car door. I basically totally flooded my car and it took years for it to dry out.

Milo says my real mistake was driving into the water. Never drive into water unless you know how deep it is and how much clearance you have under your car (ground clearance). Even a little water in the underside of your car can cause it to stall. If stalled, water can continue to rise and you can be trapped in a dire situation. Even serious off road enthusiasts will get out of their vehicles and ford a stream on foot before driving the vehicle through.

2 SPEEDING

This is really important for you new and young drivers. The last thing you want is a speeding ticket. Firstly, I think cops are more likely to stop you. Secondly, your car insurance cost will definitely increase and possibly double. Thirdly, it stays on your record for ten years. I have a lot of experience with getting caught. Chong has never gotten a speeding ticket.

I got a lot of speeding tickets in my twenties and thirties. Marie was with me on the interstate from Seattle to Vancouver when I got pulled over. My tickets for speeding mostly occurred while driving on highways. Once in the Dulles Airport Terminal I was rushing to pick up someone at the airport and got caught for speeding. That one was extra expensive.

There was a time I drove back and forth from Richmond to Roanoke a lot and I got a lot of tickets then. For one of these tickets I had to go to traffic court while I was medical school and the judge told me that he did not trust doctors anymore and then he pounded his gavel and took away my driver's license for 6 weeks. I never told my parents. When I moved to Ann Arbor, Michigan, I could not find an insurance company to insure my car because of my speeding record (remember it takes ten years for the speeding ticket to disappear). I finally found insurance, very expensive, that pizza delivery drivers use. Apparently people who deliver pizza are a poor car insurance risk.

So I can tell you that I probably drove faster than normal

people, but the real reason I got tickets is that I did not pay attention to the police cars. I would only notice them when I heard sirens blaring and saw lights flashing red in my rear mirror. Too late! Milo is really good at how to avoid speeding tickets. He has this to share with you. By the way we are not encouraging you to speed, but we are trying to help you not get tickets.

1. Police cars hide in gaps between medians on the highway and near underpasses where a road crosses above. Milo says focus your eyes on the gaps between the medians and look for the front bumper or headlight. Look for just a small piece of the police car sticking out. If you see anything like metal poking out in the gaps, don't wait to see if it is car, assume it is a police car.

2. As soon as you see a police car trying to catch speeders, immediately brake. I never did that, thinking that it was a sign of guilt. But Milo says that the police have to record a reading with radar if they are sitting still. And they have to get at least two readings at the same speed to confirm the reading is not an error. So if the first reading they get is 80 mph and the next is 78, they can't use this as evidence.

3. Watch flow of traffic. If it slows, or you see brake lights ahead, look around for why. If it seems like traffic is slowing for no reason, there could be a hidden police car. If oncoming traffic flash their high beams, they are signaling police ahead.

4. Know the unmarked police car types. Milo knows what they look like. You have to know what kind of car the police use in the state you are driving in. In the olden days they were Ford Crown Vic's in all states but now they mix it up.

5. Know the speed limit where you are driving: particularly in small towns that you are not familiar with. Really pay attention to the signs.

6. When you do get pulled over, don't be aggressive, be polite. Stay in the car. Keep your hands visible, don't be shuffling around. Some people cry, but I could never make myself cry.

Milo did get one speeding ticket that could have changed his life. He was seventeen years old driving home around midnight from his girlfriend's house on a weekday night on Smoketown Road. This road was a country road with rolling hills and no streetlights. He would speed on this road at night because you could always see if there were other cars by their headlights so he felt safe speeding. If there were cars on the road, he would slow down. If not, he would fly. So he was flying down the road when he saw way back behind him, headlights. Because of the rolling hills, the headlights popped in and out of view. So he slowed down. Well, it was a police car. He got clocked going over 75 mph in a 45 mph zone. That is reckless driving in Virginia, a misdemeanor.

He received a court date. He didn't know what to do. He was afraid to tell his parents. He did not tell his sister Kara because he thought she would immediately blab it to his parents. I asked Milo if he told anyone and he thinks he must have told his friends but he can't remember who. He was stressed out. He decided he could take care of this on his own. He would simply go to court by himself and pay the fine without telling his parents. Then one day before the court date, he wisely changed his mind and told his parents. Surprising to himself, after the initial shock, his parents focused on helping him rather than punishing him. They hired a lawyer who delayed the court date and did the legwork to discover that the police officer who gave him the ticket was not going to be nice and let him off.

If Milo had gone to court by himself, a seventeen year old boy with long, rock and roll hair, he would have been given no leniency and possible jail time. The lawyer pleaded his case, that he had a good traffic record, had good grades, and had been accepted into college. The charges were reduced. All that worry he went through. When it came down to the line, he learned his parents, more than anything, wanted to help. Still, the question up for debate is whether or not he should have slowed down because maybe the police would not have caught up to him before he turned off Smoketown Road if he had kept driving fast.

****

Remember how this book got started? As we were driving from Richmond to Ann Arbor, here is what happened. About 150 miles into the 660 mile trip I asked, "Exactly how long are you going to keep driving this car?" That's about how long it takes for my back to start hurting and I start sitting cross-legged. My mom has been asking Milo this question in her usual subtle way for about three years now, and Milo replies as he always does, "Why, there's nothing wrong with this car."

Okay, let me back up here. I can't believe what he just said. Just two nights earlier we found ourselves stranded in the parking lot of a strip mall about a mile from the Wade's house. The Mazda 6 had crawled into the parking lot fuming and making clanging sounds. Milo says he could smell burning rubber and antifreeze. And he knows what that smells like. As he lifted up the hood I told him to be careful because it can burn you if the car is overheating.

Milo says to tell you that's not true, but one should open the hood slowly to make sure nothing is spraying. You really only have to watch out when opening the radiator cap. Also, don't open the radiator cap unless the car is completely cold. Okay, I have no idea what the radiator cap is. But first he says to tell you, don't bother opening up the hood if you have no idea what you are doing. This sounds like good advice to me. So in my case, I would never open up the hood. I would call AAA. That's a 1-800 phone number on a card my parents had for us kids. It comes with automobile insurance. We have AAA as adults now.

Just in case you want to know how to open the hood in a non-

10

emergent situation, here is how you do it. There is a latch release that you have to pull before you get out of the car. It is usually lower than the dashboard on the left marked "Hood" or has a picture of a hood on it and you pull it towards you. This makes the hood rise up a bit. And then when you are standing facing the front of the car and the hood, your finger can slide under the hood til you feel the latch and then you push or pull the latch over and lift the hood. The reason the hood has an extra latch to open it is to protect the hood from accidentally flying open when the car is moving. You can imagine that, right? Not good. Then there is a stick- like thing lying along the inside of the car that you can pull up and the end of the stick fits into a spot on the interior of the hood which holds the hood up so you can let go and the hood stays open.

I try to come up with some exceptions to opening the hood in an emergency situation. "Like haven't you seen cars pulled over the side of the road with the hood up? It seems like an alert that the car is stopped and to slow down while you drive by." Milo agrees and says he thinks a car on the side of the road with the hood up means the car is broken down; send help, that the driver is not just stopping to nap.

Milo thinks some more and says, "There is only one circumstance where you could do good by lifting up the hood in an emergency situation and that is FIRE. I mean, if you could put out the fire when the car is on fire. If you had a fire extinguisher you could open the hood and put the fire out. Now this is really dangerous because the fire could burst into your face when you open the hood."

I ask him, "How would you know that the car is on fire?"

"You will see billowing black smoke." I guess there are degrees of smoke, billowing and not billowing.

Milo adds, "For sure, if looks like the car is going to explode, RUN! Don't bother trying to put out the fire. Run but if you have time, take the license plate off."

"What? Take the license plate off? Why would you do that? That doesn't make any sense." The reason for that, according to Milo, is then you can leave the car forever and no one will know it's yours and it's not your problem anymore. How did he get so wise I wonder. Maybe he saw this on the TV show "Dukes of Hazzard" or "Smokey and the Bandit."

"Wow," I thought. This man thinks of everything. This is why I was smart to marry him. So you too should pick someone smarter than yourself to be with. There are many ways to be smart. So even if you are brilliant in some ways, there will always be someone smarter in other ways and that is a good thing.

****

3 GAS

Now sometimes, being too smart can get you into trouble. I think this is the case when it comes to how Milo handles filling up the gas in his car. We had been married about seven years and I had been pumping my own gas since I was sixteen so I thought I had enough experience in this matter when something happened that shook that all to pieces.

In the 1970's there were attendants at gas stations and our parents would pull their cars to the pump and the attendant would come to the driver's side window and the driver would "roll down" (mechanically by hand) the window and say, "Fill 'er up." The attendant would also wash the windshield and ask if you wanted your oil checked. By the time we were old enough to need gas, the gas attendants were gone and it was all self-service except in New Jersey where you still have gas attendants. I think it is a state law.

When we drive together on these long road trips, Milo is the driver 99% of the time: remember my speeding problems. So Milo is the one who pumps the gas and I either wait for him or go ahead into the gas station market, use the restroom, and get Cheetos. However, this one time he really had to use the restroom so I said I would finish pumping the gas. Now I always wondered if there was something different about the way he pumped gas because he often complained about his hands smelling like gas after he fills the tank up. I just thought he was clumsy like when a person spills food a lot. I never have gas-smelly hands after pumping gas. He said I just don't notice the smell. Well after I had finished the gas fill-up and he started up the car, he looked at the gas gauge and he said, "You didn't fill the tank to full."

I said, "What? Sure I did."

He asked, "Did you click it three times"

"What are you talking about it?"

Milo said everyone clicks the pump but he doesn't know how he learned it. So when you click it three times you are really trying to fill the tank past the full mark. Note, Milo says this is not true. Why three times? Who decided that? The gas pump has an automatic shut off when the tank gets full. So what happened? Why did it stop early when I pumped the gas? The gas tank tube is narrow and the pump nozzle has a sensor such that when it senses gas backing up into the filling tube, it shuts off the flow of gas so it doesn't overflow. Milo thinks he is making sure the tank is really full by clicking three times. But I think that his hands also get gas on them from clicking three times. He does not think so.

You may wonder, why does he care that the tank is totally full? Two reasons. Milo wants to minimize having to stop and get gas. If you only fill the tank halfway, you'll have to stop again sooner to get more gas. He says there were times he had no choice because he only had enough money to fill the tank partially. He says, "But if you can squeeze just a little more gas in the tank each time you fill it, over the course of your whole lifetime, maybe you have to stop for gas less a dozen times." I wonder how much time would this really save and is it that big a deal? He also says when you are traveling long distances it can mean having to stop one less time.

I started doubting that this was a certainty: that everyone in the world but me clicks the pump three times. My second question was how does everyone learn this? How is this passed on? I know my parents did not teach me how to pump gas. I just observed what they did and I am sure my parents did not click.

By the way, the consequence of minimizing stops for gas taken to the extreme is that you will keep driving until the car is really out of gas. Does that sound smart? Women do not do this.

The second reason to fill the tank all the way is that keeping track of miles is more accurate than the fuel gauge. Let me explain. The thing that measures miles is the odometer. The odometer is on the dashboard. It keeps running total of the number of miles for the entire life of the car. In the olden days the odometer was a mechanical rotating dial and you could cheat on the number of miles by adjusting the dial. Then the car could be fraudulently represented with less miles of usage. You can imagine when the car has a lot of miles and you want to sell it used, that is not a good thing. So used car dealers would dial down the number of miles to get a better price on their used cars. Nowadays, it is a lot harder to change the miles and the odometer is a true marker for the car's mileage. In addition to total miles there is a trip odometer that you can reset to zero and measure trip distances.

So there are three ways to keep track of how long you can drive without filling up. One, the yellow warning light on the gas gauge, which, by the way did not exist when Milo and I started driving Milo says the yellow light means you are not empty, just near empty. When I see the yellow light on, I fill my tank. Another measure is the actual fuel gauge, when the needle goes to the letter "E" for empty. Milo adds that on most gas gauges the needle will fall way below the letter "E." So he waits til it is way below the "E." As a final backup measure he uses the odometer. Every time he fills the tank up, he resets the trip odometer to zero. So he knows how many miles the car went on every tank of gas. He will run the Mazda 6 to about 420 miles on the highway; 360 miles mixed city/highway leaving a half a gallon of gas in the tank. Newer cars will actually tell you how many miles you have left. Milo probably wouldn't trust it.

Another good thing about measuring how many miles you get on a tank of gas is you can calculate the miles per gallon your car gets. You know how many gallons you put in by reading the amount on the gas pump. Then you can do the math. Car companies are required to tell you the miles per gallon, mpg, each car gets. But does anybody really confirm it after they buy the car? Not me. Not ever. I think my dad asked me to do this once, but that's it. Yet you are taking for granted that you are getting the mileage they promise. In November 2014 the Department of Justice levied a harsh fine of over 10 million dollars to Hyundai and Kia for inflating their miles per gallon numbers. Testing what you are told before you believe something is always a good idea. A big gas tank on a car is a good thing because then the car has a long range. The miles per gallon times the gallon capacity equals how far the car can go.

So Milo fills the tank the same way every time. He resets the trip odometer and he pumps the tank up with three clicks. Then he can keep track by following the odometer to know how many more miles the car can go. Of course the actual miles varies depending on other factors, such as how much weight the car is carrying, aerodynamics, bike rack on top of the car, etc.

I asked a bunch of Milo's friends if they click three times and guess what, an engineer at GM said he doesn't click and sides with me. He says his logic is that he doesn't want to waste time doing the three clicks each time. He thinks over the course of his lifetime, the time he saves not clicking will counterbalance the extra time he would have to fill the tank. However, another engineer says that three clicks is standard automotive testing procedure.

Then I asked his parents. His dad said he does like I do. Milo's dad thinks there is a danger in overfilling and that comes from when he worked as a young lad pumping gas at his best friend's dad's gas station in La Crosse, Wisconsin. He and his friend were scolded if they overfilled because gas spilled on the cars. Now back then in the 1950s gas pumps did not have an automatic switch off. Milo's dad learned to listen to the sound of the gas filling and when it got close to full, the sound changed, and that's how he knew to stop.

In the end on this question, it seems there is no wrong way. Milo disagrees. What I did learn is that you can't change people's behavior because I still do it the way I do and he still does it the way he does. The other thing I learned is that when you think everyone does things the same way as you do, the odds are high that this is not so. In this way behaviors do not get questioned because everyone assumes they are doing as everyone else does. Even in the face of new ideas about why other people have a different way of doing things, people don't change the way they do it.

So how many times have I run out of gas? Never. How many times for Milo? Well as long as I have known him (about one-fifth of his life), five times and that is just on the Mazda 6. So Milo runs out of gas a lot. He never thought so until I pointed it out. Some examples: Interstate I-94 on his way to work, M14 on the way to work, the Torino going up a hill, after the Iceman bike race, and most recently, rolling down an exit ramp in the middle of Ohio. And let me tell you, Milo can tell you reasons and stories about how and why each "running out of gas event" happened.

So for you, how will you know you are out of gas? You just kind of know. The car feels like it has no energy when you apply the accelerator. Do you know what Milo does when he feels the gas is gone? He shakes the wheel a lot, real jerkily back and forth. The reason he does this is that the gas tank has a pickup at the bottom and shaking the car moves the gas around so you can eke a bit more gas in. It is like moving the drinking straw in the bottom of the glass around. But the "straw" in the car can't move so if you shake the glass you can get more fluid through the straw. Get it? At the same time he is shaking the wheel hard, he heads for the side of the road.

Then you call someone like me to bring you some gas.

Unfortunately the last time we ran out of gas, I was in the car with Milo. We were on US 23 south of Toledo, in the middle of nowhere really, and Milo exited the highway and kept the car rolling until it stopped near a house with boats, trailers, and ATVs in the yard. It looked sketchy to me but Milo said, "This looks good. They oughta have some gas cans here." Milo thought it would be better if I knocked on the door by myself. Feeling like a lost alien I approached the front door. There was a big sign alert on the window that said "No smoking! Oxygen in use." Milo says I saved him because the lady inside the house would not have opened her door to him. Fortunately, she did open her door. She was nice but looked like she had lived a tough life. I told her our plight. I could hear the TV going inside. It turned out the woman had a gas can full of gas. I didn't ask whether it was premium or regular and Milo says he would have put any kind of gas in his car at that point. So here's a case where trying to be too smart almost stranded us south of Toledo. We were knocking on strangers' doors for help.

17

Milo says I am partially to blame for this "running out of gas event" because I told him the distance to the next gas station was closer than it actually was. He says this was an error in navigation-- an entirely different topic.

I asked, "Would we have tried hitchhiking as a last resort?" It wouldn't have worked in this instance because absolutely no cars were going by where we were. Milo says no to hitchhiking, we would have called AAA.

"Wouldn't that be really embarrassing?"

"They just bring you a gas can and charge you $10 for the gas."

"Oh really? Do you know that from personal experience?"

"Remember when I ran out of gas on my way to work when I had just bought the Mazda 6? I called AAA and that is what they did."

"So you just sat there til they did?"

Should you sit in the car when you are stranded on the side of the road? Before we get to that answer, here is another instance that puts you in the same predicament.

4 FLAT TIRE

One of these days you are going to have a flat tire. Be ready for it. Guess what, you have a spare tire in your car usually. Most cars have a smaller tire, called a mini-spare, made just tough enough to drive you to a place that can sell you a new tire or fix the old one.

It happens in quick sequence. First a funny sound that you think, "Is that a flat tire?" and before you finish thinking the word "flat" the car starts to thump and jiggle. If it's the front tire, the steering wheel will start to pull funny. And then the car slows down even though you don't mean for this to happen. Fortunately every time I have been able to pull over to the side of the road. Don't stop in the middle of the road. Pull over as soon as you can; somewhere that is safe, away from traffic. Pull over as far away from the road as you can. If there are other people in the car, don't have anybody else get out of the car unless they know what they are doing. Be very careful. Don't get out of the car if cars are whizzing by you. Do not change a flat tire on the side of the road unless you are certain you are safe from oncoming traffic. I would not change the flat tire if the tire is on the side of the car nearest the road. It is dangerous to be on the side of the road. Don't keep driving, that can ruin the wheels of your car and that is not good. Only drive as far as needed to reach a safe place.

If you were in a hurry, too bad. You are in for a good two hour delay. Of course with a cell phone, you can call for help. Your parents probably have AAA and you call them for help. If you wait for help, it'll take at least one hour for someone to get to you. Every time I have had a flat tire, a kind man has stopped and then changed the tire for me. Milo says no one ever helped him when he had a flat tire. But I do know how to put the spare tire on. If you know what you are doing, changing the tire yourself will be faster than waiting for someone.

Read on the next three paragraphs if you want the basics on how to change to the spare tire. Firstly, you are probably going to get your hands and clothes a little dirty. If you are wearing a tie, take it off. Roll up your sleeves. Get out the owner's manual which is in the glovebox. Read the part about how to change a flat tire. It will tell you where to find the lug wrench, spare tire, and car lifter, known as the jack. Usually all are in the car trunk somewhere. First, you have to loosen the nuts on the wheel. Do this while the tires are still on the ground before jacking it up. Starting to take off the tire while the tire is still on the ground might seem dangerous, but the tire might spin freely once up in the air and then you would not be able to loosen the nuts.

One extra thing to know about is the wheel lock key. Some cars have this to prevent someone stealing the wheels. I learned about the lock key when I used to get my tires rotated and balanced. The tire guys would need the wheel lock key to work on the wheels every time. If one of your lug nuts looks different than the others, that means you need the lock key to put on that nut before the lug wrench will then be able to turn it. If you have a lock key but you don't know where it is, there is no way for you to get it off yourself. The tire shop people can get it off with stronger tools. I kept my lock key in the glove compartment. Sometimes it's zip-tied to the lug wrench.

So back to changing the tire, loosen all the nuts while the tire is on the ground. But just loosen the nuts a quarter turn or so. Do not remove the lug nuts yet. You use the lug wrench to loosen it. Each wheel as four or five nuts holding it on. It will be hard to turn the lug wrench at first. It always is for me. You can put the lug wrench on the lug and then put your foot on the end of the lug wrench and stand on it. To loosen, it is counterclockwise. Just remember, "Rightie tightie, leftie loosie." Milo says except some 1960's or 1970's Dodge cars but don't worry about that.

Then place the jack. Place it where the owner's manual says.

Then lift the car. Often the lug wrench is also used to turn the jack. Make sure the car is level and secure so it won't roll off of the jack. As you take off the lug nuts, make sure you don't lose them. Take the flat tire off and put the spare on. Line up the holes in the spare and put the lug nuts back in. Don't start tightening until all the lug nuts are in. Tighten evenly each lug nut a little at a time, in a star pattern. Don't tighten all the way in one shot. Tighten the lugs as best you can with the tire in the air. Then lower the car. Do the final tightening when the tire is back on the ground. No need to over tighten. Tighten fairly hard, but only as hard as you can with the wrench. Then remove the jack. The flat tire may not fit in the space that the mini-spare was stored, so just put it anywhere in the trunk or back seat.

What makes the tire go flat fast? One time, I hit a big pothole really fast and hard, on the Dulles Toll road. Within a mile or two of the pothole, the tire went flat. I was surprised by this. I did not know that the car tire could go flat by hitting a pothole hard. Other times, it has been a nail puncture.

A slow flat you can see when you look at your tires. One tire looks like it is sinking into the ground more than the rest. Some people may periodically look at their tires and check the tire pressure. That's not me. That's not Milo either as far as I know. Many times a slow flat means a nail is in the tire. When you have a nail in the tire, you can take it to a garage and they can put a plug into the hole and seal it up. Check the pressure of your spare tire once a year. Sometimes it is flat. Milo has had it where the spare was flat.

This happened the one time someone offered to help him. Milo was driving by himself from Michigan to Virginia, and on I-270 near I-81 in Maryland he got a flat. It was dark. The way Milo describes it, "A scraggly man appeared out of nowhere." I ask, "What's makes a person scraggly?"

"When it looks like the person hasn't taken a shower in a week and been sleeping under a bridge. This fella appeared from out of nowhere, up from the hillside and he offered to help. He looked like he wanted money."

Milo told him, "No thanks, I got it covered." Milo was scared of him and did not trust him to change the tire. So Milo changed to the spare alone in the dark on the side of the highway. But after he put the car down off the jack, the spare tire was squished down. It was flat too but not as flat as the other tire. And it was dark. Oh boy, what a mess. What did he do? He drove on the flat spare really slowly to the nearest open gas station. This was tough to find at night. This is why he says to check the air in your spare.

So, what to do if you are stranded? First, always try to get your car off onto the shoulder of the road. This is the part of the road to the left and/or right that is wide enough for a car but is not a traffic lane. In New England they call them break-down lanes. Then, do you get out or stay in the car? Answer: it depends on three factors, location of where you are stranded (in the road or three feet off of the road), visibility (day or night), and if a safer location exists.

1. If you can't get completely off the road and your car is on the highway blocking traffic, do not get out of your car. Do not try to cross a heavily travelled high-speed highway on foot. Stay in car. Keep seatbelts on. Keep an eye on the traffic coming from behind you.

2. If it's dark out, you really are safer in the car. Put the interior light on. This is so other cars can see your car. Emergency blinkers at night are not good because motorists coming up from behind might think the car is moving and then they might run into the back of your car.

3. Another thing to do is hang out a white cloth or piece of paper in the driver's side window. This alerts that the car is in trouble.

4. Only get out of your car if you are on the shoulder and have a safe path and place to go such as behind a guardrail. If you decide to get out of the car, get out on the side of the car away from traffic. When out of the car, do not stand in front or behind the car, where motorists can't see you.

5 DEAD BATTERY

I can guarantee this will happen to you someday unless cars move without gas power. You attempt to start the car, turn the key or push the "start" button, and nothing happens. When this happens the first thing you want to do is jiggle the steering wheel and make sure the car shift gear lever is all the way in PARK labeled "P." Then try the ignition again. If that doesn't work, step on the brake, put the car in "N" neutral and try the ignition again. If that doesn't work there is a good chance it is the battery. To check for a dead battery, turn on the headlights, and go out and look at them. If they are not on or are very dim, you have a dead battery. Possible reasons the battery dies include the headlights or interior lights left on, cold weather, alternator malfunction, or the battery is just too old. Fortunately you can jump start your car using the battery of another car. Let me forewarn you that you are playing with high power electricity here so you have to be very careful. It is kind of like Frankenstein.

You need a set of jumper cables, a car that runs, and you need to know how to open the hood of the car and keep it open. Park the two cars in such a way that the cables reach from battery to battery. In the olden days you would not want to park the cars so close that the metal bumpers touched. The battery is a plastic box with two huge battery cables attached to it, one black, one red. Black is negative and red is positive. These are the terminals. Sometimes the battery is covered and you have to take the cover off to see the terminals.

The jumper cables have metal clamps on each end and they are colored black and red also. Keep the jumper cables apart so the metal clamps don't touch each other. Have both cars with the engine off. Connect red jumper cable clamps to the red terminal of each battery first. Make sure the jumper cables' clamp bites into the metal of the battery terminal. Then connect the black jumper cable to the good car's black terminal. Finally connect the remaining black jumper cable to a thick piece of unpainted metal that is directly attached to the engine block.

This is important because when you do this last connection, there will be a spark as you connect. The spark is good because it means you have juice going, but you don't want that spark near the dead battery. Why? Because the dead battery could possibly be giving off an explosive gas.

Now start the good car. The alternator of the good car is now charging the dead battery. If the battery wasn't completely dead, it may start right away. Give it a try. If the battery was really dead, the car may not start right away. How long you charge it before you attempt to start the dead car depends how dead the battery is. Wait a minute or so, then try to start it again. If it still doesn't start, check that the cables are securely clamped to the terminals. Then try it again. After the car is started, take cables off in reverse order as you put them on. So start disconnecting the black. The black jumper cable is a grounded item and it is okay if it touches any metal. The red is hot so do not touch metal anywhere with it. Once the circuit is open, the red is no longer hot. Do not turn off the car once you get it running because it could take a few hours to completely charge up the battery.

"You can't ground a ground." Milo learned and memorized this saying from his high school auto mechanic teacher Don Dew. It helps him remember what order to connect and disconnect the jumper cables. Milo has jump-started at least a hundred cars in his lifetime he estimates. He doesn't think this is unusual. He always has jumper cables in every car. He has forgotten the jump-start events that I remember. Once we jump-started our friends Anna and Tyler's Toyota truck. Tyler said he didn't think Milo could jump-start it because nobody else could and Anna said that Milo could. She was hoping though that he couldn't because she wanted to get rid of the truck. I thought Milo could do it as well. Milo said he could jump-start anything. And he did. Another time we had made plans to meet my friend Peg after we took a communal bath at Warm Springs, Virginia, but when Peg arrived she said she needed a jump-start for her Toyota 4Runner. She had the jumper cables ready I think because she knew the battery was questionable. Another time I remember Milo helped a stranger on the road with a dead battery. We were just driving by and saw a lady standing by her car with the hood open. I watched him jump-start her car. She was really grateful. Knowing how to jump-start a car is a good skill.

****

So back to being stranded in the parking lot in the strip mall in Short Pump. Remember I was telling you about how to lift up the hood of the car? How did we get here? We had come to Richmond for Peg's dad's funeral and we had driven for 9 to 10 hours straight from Ann Arbor to the visitation without any problem. But when Milo started the Mazda 6 up in the visitation parking lot, we knew we were in trouble. It was making loud squealing noises that had no relation to wheel movement or acceleration or braking. Milo thought it was the power steering pump because he knew it was leaking and he had had to add fluid to the power steering even before we left Ann Arbor.

Note, one should never have to add fluid to the power steering so I ask again, "How many miles should you drive a car before you get a new one? When do you call it quits?" For me I have driven all my cars until I totaled the cars in accidents but that has happened only twice. So I have had only three cars.

Milo says he will keep a car until the cost of fixing it is more expensive than the car is worth. How do you know how much a car is worth? Check the blue book value. The full name is the "Kelly Blue Book" which is now easily checked online. Kelly is the name of the company that publishes the book and it was always colored blue for used car dealers. Milo says even though that sounds straightforward, dollars and cents wise, there are exceptions. For instance, when the car breaks your heart. Like when you work really hard on it and then you learn after all that there is still something else that isn't working and you realize you don't have the desire or willpower to fix it. Most people would have given up a long time before. Tenacity. This happened to Milo with his Mitsubishi Montero. Milo has a philosophy that he wants to use up the car until it can't do no more. To keep your car running til it can't do no more, he has this advice.

Maintenance Checks on the car according to Milo:

1. *Oil change every 7,000 miles.*
2. *Air filter change every 20,000 miles.*
3. *Tires change every 30,000 miles, when they are worn out.*
4. *Brake pads change every 30,000 miles. Brake rotors at the same time? Yes, but lots of people don't. That includes him.*
5. *Accessory drive belt after 30,000 miles is recommended but Milo says 50,000.*
6. *Car battery 5-7 years. You know it's weak when it seems weak on cold mornings.*
7. *Windshield wipers about once a year. If your wipers are not working great, you may not need to replace them, just clean them. Okay how do you do that? Wipe along the length of the blade with a clean coarse rag.*
8. *Make sure you always fill the windshield wiper fluid. When you run out is when you need it the most and you can't see.*
9. *Check air pressure in the spare tire once a year.*
10. *Check air pressure in tires once a month. Milo does not do this but he knows he should. You should regularly glance at your tires to make sure they don't seem low. You should know that they look like when the tires are fine so when they are getting low on air, you can tell. It is usually 30-35 psi and gas stations will have an air pump to fill the tire. You can get tire pressure gauges to check yourself. I keep one in my glove compartment, but I confess I have not used it.*

How many miles is Milo's longest driven car so far? The 1988 Mitsubishi Montero at 240,000 miles.

When I first met Milo he had three cars lined up in his driveway: the Mitsubishi Montero, the 1990 Mitsubishi Galant and the 1991 Mazda Miata. It just so happened that none of them were drivable. He says they were drivable. Drivable to go to Virginia? He says yes and no. It's just that he wouldn't do it in December. He had to borrow cars twice to drive home to his parents in Virginia for Christmas with the three cars in his driveway. Remember how I told you Milo first drove cars when he was younger than 15 years old, moving them in and out of the driveway? Twenty years later, he was still doing it, having to move two cars to get to the one in the front. The Galant lasted a little longer than the Montero. Each car had a different reason why they weren't drivable.

He also had a 1989 Ford F150 Lariat extended cab long bed. "Extended cab" means it had a second row for people to sit in and "long bed" means that the flat part of the truck was extra long. He kept it parked in the street, not in the driveway. I forgot why he kept it parked on the street, there was a good reason. He says because it was so big and took up too much room in the driveway (there were three other cars already in the driveway). He previously had a Chevy Impala that he parked in the street because it had a leak in the gas tank and it smelled like gas. I ask, "Isn't that dangerous?" He says it was not so bad. He moved the Ford F150 every once in a while because Ann Arbor has a law that parked cars can't sit in the same spot too long. Milo didn't like to park it right in front of his house. I asked him why and he said because it blocked the whole front of the house. He mostly parked it near his next door neighbors, the Seeley's, by their side yard.

I think Milo married me because I let him borrow my car when he needed to drive to La Crosse, Wisconsin to see his Grandma Bea. He needed a car that could drive that distance and he had hurt his right leg mountain biking so he couldn't drive a manual transmission (you need to push the clutch with your left foot and the brake and accelerator with your right) which is what his Miata blue convertible is. We were just acquaintances at this point.

Another moment early on in our relationship I remember is when Milo had to figure out why the ignition for the Ford F150 did not turn on the car. I think we were just friends at this point. The key would turn in the switch but it did not start the engine. I had never heard of a Ford F150 until I moved to Michigan but it has been the most sold truck in the United States for many years. You have to really get tall to climb into the pickup and then you really have to push your body up into the seat. It had a long stick shift coming out of the floor. Something I hadn't seen in a while. That seemed old fashioned to me at the time, like the school bus. Well, Milo could trick the truck into starting like people learn to steal cars by starting the ignition without a key. He would pop the hood and put a screwdriver across the terminals of the starter solenoid. That would turn on the car so he could drive it, but he wanted to fix it. Remember the Ford F150 stayed parked in the street, so Milo worked on it there. He is a car guy without a garage.

When you put the key in the ignition the key would turn freely but it would not engage the starter motor. He could feel something wasn't catching. He took off the dashboard. Our next door neighbor John often sat on his front porch with his buddy Kaz and they were out there while we were working on the truck. I literally sat in the street keeping Milo company while he was figuring it out. I like puzzles and I tried to help him figure it out. After hours passed, Kaz called me over to tell me that he was impressed that I was out there not saying much and he thought it was real nice. Kaz said, "That's the best way to help a man out, not talking too much when he's trying to work on something, but it is difficult." I always remember that now after years of marriage. I learned from Milo's dad that Milo's first girlfriend in high school sat out there for hours keeping him company as he worked on his fastback Torino. She must have really liked him.

****

6 TIRES

I became Milo's car assistant. "When do you want to change the snow tires?" I say this twice a year. Milo likes to put on snow tires because it is safer. So we go through a discussion about the snow tires. Milo says I start bringing it up around November. I want to do it sooner than he does. I like to change them while the weather is relatively good and we haven't had much snow. He wants to wait til we really need them. That is usually when it is about to get dark and it is snowing and cold. And we have to change them right then because we are going on a trip the next day. I am exaggerating a bit but you get the drift.

And so we roll out the stored tires from the shed through the back yard and then up a couple of steps onto the cement pad. And the wheels don't roll up so easily. I have just learned how to roll two at a time, each hand pushing a tire forward through the yard. Then the cement pad usually has snow on it. We bring out the lug nuts which have been stored in a bag. Did I tell you we have snow tires for two cars? So there are two bags of lug nuts. Our next door neighbor Jim once lent us a heavy weight piece of foam so Milo could put it on the cement to protect his knees from the snow. I think he kind of felt sorry for us. Milo has a very heavy car lift jack which has wheels on it that he pulls out from the shed. He also has a heavy duty lug wrench that is shaped like a giant square cross. Each tire from the shed is marked with two letters; FR, front right, RR, rear right and so on, and we place the tires around the car accordingly. Then the lug nuts get loosened. The car gets jacked up. Then he removes the lug nuts with the wrench, and after removing each one, he shakes the wrench a little to let the lug nut fall out. My job is to collect the lug nuts. Sometimes he drops them directly into my hand, sometimes he lets them drop in the cement. Sometimes they don't come all the way off the wheel, so I turn them the last turn or so myself to take them off. Sometimes he asks me to go back to the shed to pick something up. The lug nuts are usually wet so I carry them back to the shed and put them on the workbench to dry. One time I lost a lug nut in the snow. That was not good. Very stressful. Oh yeah, we lost a wheel lock key too and never found it again. They must have melted away in the snow. Or perhaps one of the squirrels found it and thought it was a nut and buried it somewhere in the yard.

After all the lug nuts (5 per wheel) are out and the new tires are in place and the new lug nuts are in place, that's 20 off and 20 on in total, we mark the tires we took off FR and so on. Then we roll these tires back to the shed. There are always 8 tires stored in the shed. We have timed it taking under one hour with both of us working together.

Milo reminded me that in addition to just changing out the lug nuts, in the spring the wheels are usually stuck to the hubs because of the salty winter. So then he has to drive the car around the block with loosened lug nuts to break the wheels free: by turning around corners very sharply. Then he drives home with loose wheels.

This past winter season, Milo did it all on his own. I think he is catching on. You see in the spring time we go through this all over again, to take off the winter tires and put on the regular tires. My vow is my next car is going to have all wheel drive and we won't have to change the tires anymore on my car.

None of your families has snow tires. You all live in warmer climates and don't have snow tires. This might be something to consider when you have a choice about where to live. Michiganders have SUV's so they get around not needing snow tires. Milo does not like SUVs.

Every couple of years I have to ask him why we can't put the snow tires on when the weather is good. Milo says, "The snow tires wear out faster when it is warm." He likes to get all the use out of each tire. Guess what that leads to...

Bald tires. If you run the tires until they wear out, the tread will disappear and you will have bald tires. This is a Milo term. He says other people use this term but I never heard of it. He says it's a common term. We have three cars so odds are high that at least one car has bald tires so we always has to figure out which car to take when it was raining or slippery. Bald tires describes the tread of the tire. If it's bald, the tread or grooves on the tire are worn flat, or almost flat. Then the tire is one smooth surface or "slick." Apparently a kind of tire on purpose with no tread is called a "slick." When it is raining, Milo would say, "Oh boy, we have bald tires." And that always makes me nervous.

The tires are very important for your safety in the car. This is how to check your tires. Turn the steering wheel so the tire is turned and get out of your car and look at the tread of the front tires. "What does tread wear look like?" New tires have a 3/4 inch deep grooves. Then it gets shallower as they wear out. There are wear bars in the tire, so when it really wears out, you can see the bars which run perpendicular to the tire. If you see smooth bars running perpendicular to the tire, all the way across the tread, you are way past needing new tires. One cool thing you can check is use a penny in the groove of the tire. Put the penny in the groove with the top of Lincoln's head first, if you can see the top of Lincoln's head, you should get new tires.

****

Because we heard the squealing sound as we pulled out of the funeral home, Milo pulled into a gas station and opened the hood. The car stopped squealing and he checked the power steering fluid level which was okay. He thought maybe whatever it was fixed itself. "Really? Do you think?" Milo thought maybe something had stuck from the heat soak after the car was turned off after the long trip down from Michigan, and then maybe whatever was stuck had freed up once we started moving again. At least that's what he hoped--still a concern.

We got back into the car and kept going. I phoned in an order for Chinese takeout at a place near the Wade's. We were fine on Highway 288. But when we got onto West Broad Street, groaning shrieking sounds, like a trapped wild animal might make, were coming out from under the hood. A whole new more awful sound. The check engine light came on and the temperature gauge was rising. Just in the nick of time we pulled into the parking lot of the strip mall with the Chinese takeout.

Milo purposely pulled into a spot which had overhead lights so you could see. When you know your car is in trouble think ahead to where you want to drive it so you have safe location, light, etc. He could have stopped earlier by the side of the road but that would have been dangerous because it would have been in the way of traffic and dark.

Milo popped the hood and then he smelt antifreeze. You should never smell antifreeze because it is normally in a sealed system. I got out of the car and went to get the Chinese food.

When I came back with the Chinese food, I found a sad Milo by the car and he said, "This might be the end."

****

7 HOW TO BUY A USED CAR

Remember I mentioned Milo had his first car right away and he drove it to high school every day? This is how he got it. He saw this cool car out in an empty lot near where he lived. He knew what kind of car it was just by looking at it. It was a 1968 Torino GT fastback. I think it was a kind of muscle car. And it had nice wheels and fresh paint. He found another car, a 1969 Torino GT fastback, in the newspaper classified ad section. So he had a choice between these two cars.

Milo went to test drive the car from the newspaper with his dad. When they showed up at the owner's house, it was already warmed up, engine running and ready to drive. This was a bad sign. And Milo knew this. This could have meant the car didn't start well. That means trouble right away. And then when they hopped in the car for the test drive, the owner drove the car with Milo and his dad as passengers. He wouldn't let Milo drive the car. Now Milo was only 16 years old, maybe the owner thought Milo would not be careful enough. So they drove around the block. Suddenly a sound, "Pp...ppppopo.. pooo.. pooop," came out of the car. The owner jumped out of the driver's seat with a spark plug wrench ready in his hand, popped the hood open before Milo and his dad could get out of the car, grabbed the hot spark plug, and quickly tried to screw it back into the hot engine before anyone would notice. But of course Milo was quick and knew what was going on. This was the slightly more expensive car (1200 vs 800 dollars) that

Milo says now looking back that he should have bought.

Wow. Can you imagine? This is nuts to me. After a test ride like that. This car clearly had issues and yes the owner did drive around with a spark plug wrench but the owner would not budge on the price. Now about thirty-three years later, Milo says, "But let me tell you, that car was a completely untouched survivor fastback Torino."

"A survivor, what do you mean?"

"A survivor doesn't mean it still runs. A survivor means no one has replaced anything. That it is an original." Milo adds, "It was a big block car 429."

"Big block 429? What does that mean?"

The number indicates the cubic inches displacement of the engine and something 300 is small block and 400 is big block. So the bigger the number, the larger the engine. Displacement is the volume displaced by the moving pistons. It is a measure of volume. The engine block is a big mass of metal. Milo says these survivor-type cars now would go for 50 grand.

Then they test drove the other car, the 1968 Torino that was nicely painted and had nice wheels. Milo drove it a couple of times and Milo decided. His parents bought the 1968 Torino. Milo is sure his dad told him he was crazy but they bought it anyway.

Now Milo realizes he chose the wrong one. He realizes he bought the newer looking one and the cheaper one. At that time it sure seemed like a lot of money. But Milo had no idea that the car he bought had a radiator with holes in it and that the transmission and the engine had major mechanical issues until he drove it for a few days. Within the first week the car kept overheating. This car, if you can believe it, only got 6 or 8 miles per gallon. Boy he sure wasted a lot of leaded gas (that's what the gas was back then) which caused a lot of pollution which he says he is sorry for. Back then nobody talked or cared about pollution or energy conservation. At least no one we knew.

So there are many good reasons to never buy a new car. A new car immediately depreciates in value as soon as you drive it. So let us help you make a good choice if you want to buy a used car. Milo recommends looking on Craigslist and eBay. Buy from a private seller, don't go to a car dealer. The reason for that is you get the best deal from a private seller. The car dealer adds to the purchase price on top of what the car is worth. A one owner car is good. Cars from states with lots of snow are not good because these states use salt to the roads in winter and cars rust. Make an appointment to look at the car, and take someone you know that's a car person with you. Try to catch the person selling the car off guard with a question like "Why are you selling it?" Really see if they seem honest when answering the question.

When you look at the car, look for signs of an accident. Every car has a VIN number. With the VIN number you can look up reports if it has been in an accident. If the car has had a major insurance claim, it will trigger a report. Don't buy a car if it has been in an accident. A repainted car has been in an accident. The repainted car will show a difference in color from new to old paint and you can see overspray. Look for overspray in places like the door openings, called door jambs, and on the rubber seals that surrounds the windows and doors.

Test drive the car and flip every switch to make sure they work. Do not have the radio on at first. Listen to the car while you drive; feel how it turns, accelerates, and brakes. Then turn on the radio and see what kind of radio stations are on the presets. If it is heavy rock and roll, the car has been run hard. If it is classical and jazz, maybe the car has been treated nicely. Milo recommends a mechanical inspection before you buy it, so take it to someone you know who can do that. Milo can do that, or take it to a garage. Any garage will do it for a small fee.

First and foremost, do not pay the asking price of the car. Start bargaining, twenty percent lower than you want to pay.

One time Milo went to look at a 1980's BMW 5-series, a car he always wanted. The car looked nice, clean, and was an interesting dark orange color he'd never seen. The owner said the car had been brought in from out of the country. Suspicion #1.The owner also wanted only cash and right away. Suspicion #2. The car was also parked in front of a house in a nice suburb, but the house looked nearly empty. Suspicion #3. All these things seemed to add up to trouble, so Milo passed on this car.

He also looked at many really beat up pickup trucks before he bought the Ford F-150. Milo says to be patient and wait for what you want and what feels right.

The procedure for purchasing a used car from an individual

varies depending on the state you are in. They all require a transfer of title. The title is a piece of paper that you keep in your basement somewhere. It has the VIN number on it. Make sure the VIN number on the title matches the VIN number on the car. The VIN number can be found on a plate mounted on the dashboard on the driver's side of the car visible through the windshield. It is the legal identity of the car. You have to have the title. Read the title; if it has a clear title, there is no lien. The title will say if there is a lien. If it says there's a lien, then you can't get insurance on the car without the title being cleared. A lien means the car is not the owner's entirely, that there is a loan on the car, so the title will say the name of the loan company or bank that has the lien. Some states you can sign the title over to the next owner. Some states you have to go the DMV (Department of Motor Vehicles) with the previous owner/seller and do a title transfer.

So if you decide instead that you want to buy a new car and you still have your old car, you will make more money if you sell it yourself. Do not go to the dealer thinking to trade in your old car and how great that is. It is a rip off. The dealer will not pay you as much for your old car compared to what you can get selling yourself. Most of your parents do the trade-in at the dealer because it is easier that way. If you choose to sell it yourself, you have to make time to have people test out your car and then haggle over the price. So you can make the call what your time is worth.

Milo has lots of experience buying used cars so he is a great resource for you.

****

Secretly I was pleased. I thought, "Maybe we can get a new car right now and drive it home to Ann Arbor." But Milo was very upset. He had found the engine was very hot, overheating, and there was antifreeze spilling out of the overflow tank. So then he thought the water pump failed because the water pump normally circulates the antifreeze. So he thought it could be the end because if the cooling failed, overheating the engine would have irrevocably damaged the engine.

Then I called Milo's dad. Paul Wade picked us up. We loaded our luggage into Paul's car. Milo wrote a note that he left on the Mazda 6 saying the car was broken and that he would return the next morning to move it.

The rest of the evening, Milo could not relax. He was thinking of who to call and what to do. We were supposed to leave for Ann Arbor soon because we both had to go back to work. I was fine. I enjoyed the Chinese food. Paul Wade had a mechanic he recommended. Milo was thinking up persuasive stories to get a mechanic to work on the car first thing in the morning. Milo knew he wouldn't have time to fix the car himself, and it might be too big of a job. The only good news was that the mechanic was close, so Milo could drive the car there in the morning, the car wouldn't need to be towed. You can drive a car a short distance after it's overheated, if you let the car cool down first.

The next morning Milo and his dad went back to the Mazda 6. Milo opened the hood and looked again. He found the belt that spins the water pump had come off its pulley, which would explain *the overheating. He took the plastic cover off the engine and immediately inspected the water pump. It was spinning freely and seemed to be in working order. Then he noticed the tensioner pulley, a pulley that is spring loaded to push on the water pump belt to keep it tight, was melted and its bearings were seized. So then Milo thought, "Great news. I just need to replace the pulley." When he looked on online on his iPhone in the parking lot, he learned that this pulley was prone to failure, and that Mazda had stopped using it on newer cars. The Mazda 6 owners' online forum had this information. Mazda did a work-a-round and used a different belt which was not commonly used in many cars. It is stretched onto the pulleys, rather than using a tensioner. Milo found the part on the shelf of the local auto part shop and put it in. It cost something like $15 dollars. He started the car and everything was fine, the overheating had not damaged the engine. Crisis averted again. Milo and his Dad were home in time for breakfast, and even before I was awake.*

A year later in 2015, I ask "So when are you really going to get a new car?" The Mazda 6 windshield has been cracked since we have been married and finally he is willing to replace the windshield because it really has gotten two cracks and they are spreading. Milo holds off on replacing the windshield because he knows the replacement windshield will not be as good as the original and it won't seal as well as the factory installed windshield. I pursued my line of questioning and asked, "What if it needs a new clutch or new transmission?" He said that would not necessarily mean he would get a new car.

By the way he is still having to refill the power steering fluid because it is leaking and we don't know why.... I almost have to scream, "So really when would you 100 % get a new car?"

He calmly replied, "When it throws a rod."

"What is that?"

Cars have 4, 6, or 8 cylinders. Each cylinder has a connecting rod which connects the piston to the crankshaft. It is piece under a lot of strain. Eventually if the car is driven way longer than anyone would, the rod breaks in half and busts through the engine and metal flies out. That is "throwing a rod." Okay that sounds final. So now I understand how far Milo is willing to keep going. And our story ends here.

****